VOICES
TO
Our Children

Old Sayings and Everyday Affirmations
"Wisdom and Nuggets for Today's Youth"

Published by:
Taylor-Made Publishing
P.O. Box 364
Pearland, TX 77588
jt1288@aol.com

Packaging/Consulting
Professional Publishing House
1425 W. Manchester Ave. Ste B
Los Angeles, California 90047
323-750-3592
Email: professionalpublishinghouse@yahoo.com
www.professionalpublishinghouse.com

Editor: Dianne Taylor
Cover Design: Kevin Allen
Cover Layout: Professional Publishing House
Formatting: Professional Publishing House
Third Printing November, 2024
10 9 8 7 6 5 4

ISBN 978-0-9720645-0-4

For inquiries contact: Taylor-Made Publishing, P.O. Box 364,
Pearland, TX 77588, Email: jt1288@aol.com

VOICES
TO
Our Children

Old Sayings and Everyday Affirmations
"Wisdom and Nuggets for Today's Youth"

STEPHEN TAYLOR

Taylor-Made Publications
Anaheim, California

DEDICATION

This book is dedicated to all those who have contributed to my growth from childhood into manhood. I listened to a countless number of people, some I knew, others I heard in passing, and others I aspired to be like. My biggest supporter was my grandmother Helen Spicer, whom I address as "Mama." Mama raised me through my formable years and always talked about opportunity. She felt opportunity only came once in a lifetime, and she wanted me to be prepared when it presented itself. "When the door of opportunity opens," as Mama referred to it, "go through it before it closes." I watched her feed the homeless (who we refer to as "hobos") even though we were on government assistance. She provided a safe haven for all of us and those who needed it. She was extremely proud of her own biological children and felt I had something special. My twin sister Stephanie and I were protected by Mama. Those around her knew she treated us differently than her adult children and other grandchildren. Mama would encourage us to take advantage "of the gifts from God."

Because I had such a positive relationship with my grandmother "Mama," I wanted to share something with my son that he could cherish and pass down to his offsprings. When I was growing up, the things that the elders would say to us during normal conversations, we called them "old sayings." Today people refer to these "sayings" as affirmations. Originally, I wanted my son to remember these words as Voices to My Child, as well as other children.

My wife, Dianne had other ideas. She insisted that I rename the book so all those who read it would make a connection to it. When I began to think about it she was absolutely right, because this book was written on the premise to share and give back some of life's little things that we sometimes fail to remember. After all, parents are always searching for words to share with their child/children to help them better understand life experiences.

With that being said, I introduce to you *Voices to Our Children*.

ACKNOWLEDGMENTS

I know if I begin to recognize all those who have influenced me by name, I will inadvertently leave someone out. I will make an honorable attempt to include all by keeping it simple. I must begin by acknowledging the only mother I have ever known, my grandmother whom I call "Mama," Helen Spicer.

From her I learned that the most important virtue of life is the gift of giving. I watched her give without reservation, expecting nothing in return. Those of us who were touched by her have passed on this gift to our children by our actions. It's my hope that they will continue to share this gift with their offsprings. I also know the challenges they face are much more different than ours because this is the "gimme" generation.

My wife, Dianne, has played a pivotal role in all my accomplishments as an adult and has reinforced all eight sections in the Table of Contents throughout my life. Her guidance and love has made this book possible for all to read and cherish.

Jordon, our son, is the reason why this book was written. I wanted to leave him and hopefully his children and his children's children my thoughts on certain aspects of life. I began leaving him morning notes that we refer to as affirmations. These notes were *"Wisdom Nuggets"* to start his day with a powerful, positive tone.

I want to pay tribute to my sisters, brothers, aunts, uncles, cousins, friends, teachers, professors and acquaintances. This book is a product of those who came into my life at one point or another. I've taken something away from all of you.

Thank you.

TABLE OF CONTENTS

Introduction 11

Will Power 13

Inspirations... 27

Education.. 41

Organization 53

Sports 61

Accomplishments.. 75

Love 89

Life's Gifts.. 109

INTRODUCTION

Voices to Our Children is written in an easy to read format which can be completed in one sitting if you choose to do so. It is an idea read for both young and mature adults to enjoy throughout the day whether at school or work. At times the book appears to lean toward the male gender because it was written to our son. I assure you male and female, young and old can benefit. This is a great uplifting book to motivate young people and adults.

As I was writing *Voices to Our Children*, there were a few days when I did not leave a note. Jordon, my son, would come to me and ask, "Where are the notes?" From that day on, I believe I had reached him and that he was gaining inspirational insight from what he read. As you will notice in the Table of Contents, there is a section titled "Sports." I included this section because at one time he played baseball, basketball, and football. And, as we all know, just like life, playing sports can bring ups and downs that can sometimes have you doubting yourself. He eventually concentrated on one sport--baseball before graduating from high school. He is currently playing college baseball in southern California.

I encourage you to find a quiet setting and begin reading these little nuggets and share them with others. Or, you can do as I did. Write one a day on a sheet of paper and leave it for your son or daughter to read. If he or she has questions, please discuss it with them.

I believe that, you, along with your loved ones will take away something new and different each and every time you read *Voices to Our Children*.

WILL POWER

*Will power is your tour guide
to your accomplishments*

WILL POWER

Will power is your mental and physical force that you expose to the world.

Will power is total control of your being.

Will power is the electricity within your circuit.

Will power is your own personal decision.

Will power is your ability to challenge yourself and others.

Will power is the act to carry out your commitment.

Will power is an unwritten document declaring your declaration to excel.

Pray for will power!

COURAGE

Courage is the first step for mankind.
Courage gives you moral strength.
Courage is your performance on stage that demands a curtain call.
Courage is the challenge within you.
Mentally confident is a gift from courage.
Make sure your backbone absorbs courage.
Courage gives you personal achievement.
Courage is a court trial within you without a jury.
Pray for courage.

COURAGE

Courage is your most integral thoughts put into actions.
Courage is a mirror that reflects your fortitude.
Courage is your own experiences and challenges that give
you the backbone to face adversities.
Courage will come in many forms of bravery.
Courage is a test of will power.
You must have a purpose to have courage.
Keep courage personal and close to the heart.
Courage is an achievement through unfavorable odds.
Pray with courage!

AMBITION

Ambition is the heart beat of your accomplishments.

Ambition is your searchlight running through the fog.

Ambition is not measured in fame and fortune only.

Ambition takes effort and love for your dreams.

Ambition should never be ruthless.

Ambition gives you power to succeed.

Make your ambitions clear, deliberate, and precise.

Be eager to pray!

AGGRESSIVENESS

Take charge of your life.

The early bird catches the worm.

React to the things that affect you.

Don't hesitate; you could be left behind!

Prioritize your daily activities.

Attack your problems head on.

Control your surroundings.

Make all your duties important no matter what.

Build a solid foundation to stand on.

Pray for your stability!

DECISIONS

All decisions aren't good decisions.
Your decision is your word.
A decision is your obligation to fulfill your judgment.
A decision is when you make up your mind to perform.
Decisions should be made after careful consideration.
A decision is a victory of the mind.
Firmness and character are always involved in a decision.
A decision is the final call.
Decide to pray!

SACRIFICE

Sacrifice is to give up something that you value.

Sacrifice is to compromise and gain advantage with your goals.

Sacrifice is the battle between *the haves and the have-nots.*

Sacrifice is a decision to see how bad you want it.

Sacrifice is devoted to a greater value.

Sacrifice is your choice to offer yourself exclusively.

Make time to pray!

DESIRE

If you want something, get it.

Desire is determination.

Desire is purpose.

Desire is your intention to succeed.

Your heart and desire work together.

Desire is a direction with a map.

Desire is working toward a goal.

Prayer is deserving!

TAKE CHARGE

Take charge of your life.

Take charge in the classroom, on the field, and at work.

Command the best from yourself and others.

Your leadership is required.

Make sure you are the best man for the job.

Respect will come by making leaders not followers.

It's your job, believe me, others will want it.

If you uplift those who are behind you, you uplift yourself.

Move forward with confidence. It rubs off.

Take charge with prayer!

FOCUS

Focus is your center of attention.

Focus is your ambition to seek the known and the unknown.

Focus is your challenge within to produce results.

Focus is concentration on one or many objectives.

Focus is your hidden substance.

Focus is your thought before action.

Focus is an affair with the mind to conduct performance.

Focus on Prayer!

NEVER GIVE UP

You are the king of your castle.

Always find a way to accomplish your dreams.

Don't let age, height, weight, strength, looks, or anything defer your dreams.

Eliminate your mental weakness and improve your actions.

Stay on the front line.

Be anxious about life and what it offers.

Never give up on the game. It's all around you.

Never give up praying!

INSPIRATIONS

I want to be like . . .

OPPORTUNITY

Mama would always say, "Opportunity only comes once. Don't let the door close behind it."

Opportunity is your knight in shining armor. Take advantage of it.

Hard work creates opportunities.

Opportunity is never given. It's earned.

Opportunity presents itself when someone notices you.

You never know when an opportunity will come.

Don't wait for an opportunity—make opportunities.

All doors can lead somewhere. Make the right choice.

Prayer is an opportunity!

OPPORTUNITY

Opportunity is not luck. You deserve it.

Opportunity is goals put into action.

Take advantage of every opportunity. It's in your favor.

Opportunity is your chance or time; either expected or unexpected.

Opportunity is a celebration of your dreams.

Opportunity is a victory.

Opportunity will always have a risk.

Opportunity is an asset that counts.

Every prayer is an opportunity!

BELIEF

BELIEVE IN YOUR EXISTENCE.

BELIEF IS A PROMISE TO YOURSELF CALLED TRUST.

BELIEF IS YOUR MOUNTAIN TO CLIMB WITH PLENTY OF PIT-FALLS.

BELIEF IS THE FINAL VERDICT.

WE INVEST IN OUR BELIEFS.

YOU HAVE REACHED A MILESTONE WHEN OTHERS BELIEVE IN YOU AND YOUR ABILITIES.

THERE IS NO ROOM FOR DOUBT WHEN YOU BELIEVE.

BELIEF IS THE STRENGTH AND MUSCLES IN YOUR THOUGHTS.

LEADERS ARE CHOSEN BECAUSE OF THEIR BELIEFS.

MAKE GOOD DECISIONS BECAUSE IT'S YOUR BELIEF.

BELIEVE IN PRAYER!

HEROES

A HERO IS A PERSON WHO CAN IMPRESS YOU.

YOUR GREATEST HEROES ARE YOUR PARENTS, GUARDIANS, AND LOVED ONES.

YOUR NOBILITY AND ACHIEVEMENTS DISPLAY QUALITIES OF A HERO.

A HERO WILL RESCUE YOU.

FRIENDS ARE TRUE HEROES WITHOUT A TITLE.

ONE OF YOUR GOALS SHOULD BE A HERO TO SOMEONE ELSE.

A HERO IS YOUR OWN PERSONAL LEGEND.

A TRUE HERO IS UNAWARE OF HIS DEEDS.

HEROES PRAY!

PATIENCE

Patience is truly a virtue.

A tolerant and understanding person will go a long way.

Patience is working a problem from the beginning to the end.

Patience is demonstrating your calmness through the storm.

Patience hides your complaints in despair.

Patience is waiting for the right moment.

Patience is restraint under pressure.

Prayer teaches you patience!

IDENTITY

Never lose sight of yourself.

Remember where you came from.

It's easy to associate yourself with something different, just don't forget your values.

You are a member of a race of people called the human race.

Your position should always be to preserve your ancestral heritage and pass on your knowledge to others.

Identity is your ownership and recognition.

Identity establishes your personality and character.

Your identity is your trademark.

Your identity should embrace a reflection of your behavior.

The quality of your identity is rooted in your upbringing.

If you change, your identity changes.

Affiliate yourself with prayer!

I'M SORRY

You should say it and mean it.

I'm sorry is regretting something out of character.

I'm sorry is difficult to say, but more difficult if you don't say it.

Most people will appreciate and accept an apology.

You grow from every mistake when you acknowledge it.

Always be bigger than your mistake with an apology.

You become small when you don't recognize your mistakes.

Make sure I'm sorry is a mistake and not a gesture.

Don't use anger as an apology. Just don't say it.

How many times do you say I'm sorry?

Are you really sorry?

Praying offers forgiveness!

FIRST IMPRESSIONS

Your image can make you or break you.

Your first impression begins your life story.

Your first impression will demand attention, like it or not.

Make sure your impression has a style that is associated with remarkable character.

You are always selling yourself.

A perception of you is seen through others' eyes.

Stay natural.

Prayer will keep you humble!

FIRST IMPRESSIONS

It may not be fair because people judge you on sight.

Don't leave home without looking your best.

When you speak, make sure you capture the attention of the person to whom you are speaking to.

Your imprint is what people are looking for.

If someone copies you, be flattered.

Portray yourself to the utmost.

Never lose sight of your beginnings.

People feed off your image, so be productive.

Remain unique, pray!

FEAR

It's the fear of failure that stops your dreams.

You will never fail if you attempt to live out your dreams even if you don't accomplish your goals.

Fear should never enter your soul.

Fight fear with hard work.

Don't ever be afraid to be yourself.

Stand up and be counted.

Don't be terrified to express yourself when it counts.

The only danger in fear is letting it control you.

Don't let life pass you by because of fear. You can lose your dreams.

Fear no man, pray!

BE POSITIVE

Being positive creates positive results.

You have a better outlook on life.

Positive things happen.

Life is happier.

Everyday is a rewarding day.

Nothing can stop you.

The impossible is possible.

You love yourself and respect others.

You become a leader – the captain of your ship.

You have positive results when you pray!

POSITIVE THINKING

Yes, I can.

Yes, I can be the number one draft choice.

Yes, I can be an A – B+ student.

Yes, I can be the person I want to be.

Yes, I can be confident about myself.

Yes, I can be determined to accomplish my goals.

Yes, I can be successful in my career.

Yes, I can be motivated in my progress.

Yes, I can be driven to complete my task.

Yes, I can possess all my dreams.

Yes, I can be in control of my future.

Yes, I can pray!

EDUCATION

The Key to Your Existence

EDUCATION

Life's journey becomes easier with a solid education.

Let your education work for you.

Elementary and high school is only the beginning.

Listen, learn, and participate is essential to discovering yourself.

You should always share what you learn.

There is no monopoly on knowledge.

Be aggressive to learn and teach.

Your mental capacity is your treasure.

You owe yourself more than anyone else.

Prayer is the answer!

EDUCATION

Education is the support you need to establish your future.

Education is the place to train your mind.

Education is a crystal ball that can predict your future.
Take advantage of every educator, they are specialists.

Whatever it takes, cultivate your skills.

Having an education is a process of learning that no one can
ever take.

Your knowledge should not be replaced. It should be shared.

Educate yourself through prayer!

SCHOOL/COLLEGE

The true meaning of school is to listen, learn, and participate.
School is the world in a classroom.
School is your training ground "to be all you can be."
Finishing school is a great achievement—not going is a personal punishment.
Listen and you will overcome your shortcomings.
Learn and you will never be a step behind.
Participate and share your knowledge and dreams.
Pray that you finish!

FIRST DAY OF SCHOOL

LISTEN, LEARN, AND PARTICIPATE.

IT'S YOUR YEAR TO EXCEL.

STAY AHEAD OF THE GAME.

PERFORM AT THE HIGHEST LEVEL.

YOUR BEST CAN ALWAYS BE BETTER.

TAKE ACTION TODAY.

FULFILL YOUR ACADEMIC DREAMS.

PRAY FOR SUCCESS!

HOMEWORK

Homework is practice. The more you do it, the better you become.

When it gets hard, you work harder.

When you get tired, you work harder.

When you want to stop, you continue until it's done.

Homework rewards you with knowledge.

Don't quit.

Knowledge is power so pray!

TESTS

A test is a summary of everything you have learned.
A test is an opportunity to respond to your hidden talents.
A test shows your knowledge on paper.
A test is an examination on trial.
A test is a chance to respond to your critics.
A test is a great day for achievement.
Begin your test with a prayer!

GRADES

Grades are the essence of success.

Good grades give you wisdom and direction.

Grades are a mark on your character.

Good grades can open the door to your future.

When you think school is difficult, you lose sight of your grades.

Start with good study habits.

Sacrifice 12 years plus college or suffer for 60 years of your life—you make the choice.

Prayer can answer all doubts!

GRADES

GRADES ARE A REFLECTION
OF
YOURSELF.
NO ONE CAN EVER TAKE
AWAY
GOOD GRADES.
GOOD GRADES BUILD
SELF-ESTEEM.
PRAYER CAN HELP YOU REACH YOUR SCORE!

SENIOR YEAR

PLAN YOUR FUTURE.

LEAD BY EXAMPLE.

YOU HAVE CLASSMATES THAT ADMIRE YOU.

THIS IS A MEMORABLE YEAR.

IMAGE BUILDING CAN GO A LONG WAY.

STAY ON TOP, IT CAN EASILY SLIP AWAY.

TAKE CHARGE, YOU DESERVE IT.

YOUR LAST YEAR MEANS EXCELLENT PERFORMANCE

"DO THE RIGHT THING!"

SENIORS PRAY TOO!

LEARNING

Never stop the process of learning.
An essential part of learning is listening.
Always remember what you have learned.
Learning has the ability to fix problems.
Everyday acquire something new to take with you.
Keep your memory sharp. It's always useful.
Learning is to be informed.
Wisdom is what you obtain by learning.
Count your smallest skill.   It's worth it.
Learn to pray!

ORGANIZATION

Mindful Thinking

ORGANIZATION

Organization is purpose or work.

Organization is action taken to maintain order.

Organization creates direction to follow in your course of life.

Organization makes adjustments easy.

Organization is scholarly knowledge of location or position.

Organization is individual awareness.

Organization is systematically smart.

Organization is your step-by-step formula.

Organization is power and strength.

Schedule time to pray!

PREPARATION

Preparation is 90% of the outcome.
"Be prepared" is the motto of the Boy Scouts.
Preparation is an experience made easy.
Preparation is the rule not the exception.
Given things are equal, prepare and make them unequal.
Preparation is a plan for success.
Preparation is your roadmap that guides you down the right
path to accomplish your dreams.
You prepare everyday for something.
Preparation is getting ready for a purpose.
Preparation is your basic training.
Prepare for the unknown with prayer!

PLANNING

A daily plan brings order to your life.

An organized man is a smart man.

Don't leave home without your plan.

You are always ahead of the ball game when you plan.

The future becomes brighter when you know beforehand . . . that's planning.

Your accomplishments are endless with a systematic plan.

Make time for your planned details. It pays off.

Plan to pray!

EXPERIENCE

One of our goals in life is to gain experience.

Don't let impatience get in the way of experience.

Take advantage of your mentors.

Longevity equipped with knowledge and skill equals experience.

Mistakes, setbacks, faults, gains, minuses, flaws, accomplishments are your experiences.

Let experiences turn into future success.

Everyone's experience is different -- learn from others.

Gain experience through your parents. Just listen.

Be objective and let it come in.

A thief can never take away your experiences.

Experience prayer!

CONSISTENCY

Consistency is the key.
Consistency will always put you in a winning position.
Consistency is keeping the same schedule for success.
Consistency is an agreement to stand firm.
Consistency shares your principles with the world.
Consistency has no room for contradiction.
Consistency is harmony without music.
Be consistent and pray!

SPORTS

Determine the Outcome

I am better than the best

Why?

I know it!

WINNERS

Winners never quit,

And

Quitters, never win.

I will never quit!

I am a winner!

Win with a prayer!

WINNERS

Winning is an attitude.
You can win even if the scoreboard doesn't say it.
Winners take chances.
Winning is capturing the moment.
Achieving victory is not without struggle.
Winning is earned.
Loyalty and affection shadows a winner.
Winners battle to capture success.
Fame is the reward.
Competition creates the climate to victory.
A winner prevails even through difficult times.
Triumph through prayer!

PLAYING SICK

If you decide to play when you are sick

You play

Harder,

Smarter,

More aggressive,

Bold and active.

You don't play like you are sick.

Pray for good health!

PRACTICE

Be prepared.

Set goals.

Show pride.

Never give up.

Be positive.

Make results.

Love your progress.

Never forget how you made it.

Start practice with a prayer!

WIN YOUR POSITION

REMAIN FRIENDS AND COMPETE.

SOMEONE WANTS YOUR SPOT, SO SECURE IT.

ONE BIG PLAY DESERVES ANOTHER.

COMPETE WITH AUTHORITY.

TAKE POSSESSION WITH FAIR PLAY.

A DOMINANT BAT AND GREAT DEFENSE TELLS THE STORY.

PLACE PRAYER AT THE TOP OF YOUR LIST!

ON TOP

It's hard to reach the top.

It's harder to stay on top.

Don't ever fall from the top.

You can never rest once you've reached the top.

Always strive to do better.

Continue to work on perfection and you will always stay on top.

You're always on top with a prayer!

CHALLENGE

Never be content.

Challenge yourself to be better.

Do the extra work.

Make your effort special.

Win the duel in your mind.

Never be satisfied.

Don't challenge prayer!

GAME DAY

Stay focus.
Big hits, no errors.
Be better than your best.
Hit, run, and score.
Win! Baby Win!
Develop a winner's attitude.
Remember, every cage can be rattled.
Whatever you do, prove that you are the best.
Walk on the field with pride, and leave with dignity.
Praying is part of winning.
Score with a prayer!

GAME DAY

Big hits, no errors.
Your day to show your talent.
Great practices equal great games.
Approach every game with a plan.
Play to win.
Make others play better.
Take ownership.
Make your presence known.
Expose your talents.
Make your team better.
Performance speaks for itself.
The bat and glove earn respect.
Play to be a leader.
Are you game enough to pray?

THE 3 C'S

Confidence, Concentration, Commitment, and Sportsmanship.

Confidence is a reflection of your preparation.

Concentration is the invisible engine which idols without interruption.

Commitment is the driving force behind your accomplishments.

Sportsmanship is the glue that oversees the 3 C's and keeps the game in prospective.

Make an impact and pray!

ACCOMPLISHMENTS

Success is what you make it

SUCCESS

Success equals,

Hard work,

Harder work,

Hardest work.

There is no other choice.

Use prayer as a tool!

SUCCESS

Success is your personal measurement you set for yourself.

Success is your desire to achieve.

Prosperity is a successful outcome.

Your devotion will bring about fame.

Success is obtaining something . . . you name it.

Success offers many benefits.

It's your duty to be successful.

Make success an addiction.

Successful people pray!

HARD WORK

You can never replace hard work.

There is no substitute for hard work.

Society will appreciate your work ethics.

Be an example to those who look up to you.

Hard work can be both physical and mental.

Your performance is a result of hard work.

Workmanship is ownership.

Your biggest payday will come from hard work.

Reward yourself by praying!

DETERMINATION

Determination is the motor that will not allow you to stop.

Determination is a decision that keeps you going.

Determination is your purpose for completion.

Determination qualifies you to start and finish.

Be determined to find out who you are.

Be determined to settle for the best.

Determination is to go the extra mile.

Determination is the deciding factor.

Prayer can determine the answer!

ASPIRATION

ASPIRATION IS YOUR ULTIMATE DESIRE FOR YOURSELF.

ASPIRATION IS YOUR ENERGY WITHIN TO SOAR ABOVE THE REST.

ASPIRATION IS THE MOVEMENT OF YOUR LIFE.

ASPIRATION IS THE FINISH LINE YOU HAVE AIMED TOWARDS.

ASPIRATION IS EVERYTHING YOU DREAMED AND WORKED FOR.

ASPIRATION IS YOUR ENDEAVOR TO ADVANCE.

ASPIRATION IS THE ONLY TIME YOU SHOULD BE SELFISH.

PRAYER IS ASPIRING!

ACHIEVEMENT

*A*CHIEVEMENT EQUALS,

*H*ARD WORK,

*D*ESIRE,

*D*EDICATION,

*S*ACRIFICE,

*A*ND BELIEF,

*N*OT LUCK.

*P*RAYER IS YOUR NEXT STEP!

ACCOUNTABILITY

Your word is a moral contract.
As you mature, you become more responsible.
True men want to be accountable.
Accountability is truly an award to cherish.
Your personal quest is wrapped around accountability.
Someone will always count on you.
Accountability is your payment to society.
Accountability challenges your creditability.
When you count your blessings you become accountable.
Accountability is responding to your agreement.
Always count on prayer!

VOTE

Your vote will always count, win or lose.
You vote for your future.
Your ancestors and forefathers fought and died for you to have the right to vote.
Voting is necessary for change.
Your vote is a formal expression of the issues that affect you.
Your vote is your right to participate and endorse.
Casting your vote is your recorded support.
Voting is a nameless ballot with overwhelming consequences.
Voting does not require specific talents.
Elect to pray!

NEGOTIATION

The art of negotiation.

Stand firm.

Be direct.

Keep eye contact.

Sell yourself.

Remain confident.

You control the conversation.

Win!

Praying is not negotiable!

EXPECTATION

Expectation is the requirement that you place on yourself.

Expectation is an obligation to live up to.

Expectation is your determination to gain your desire.

Expectation is your insight without doubts.

Expectation is looking forward to your plan.

Expectation is an idea for the future.

You're expected to be noticed.

Prayer is expected!

DREAMS

Everyone has dreams.

What are you going to do about yours?

Dreams come true only if you want them to.

Dreams can be your future so plan and prepare.

Dreams are your mental secret waiting to become reality.

Make your dreams work for you.

Goals are dreams. Make your plan.

Dreams are simple.

Accomplishing your dreams require work.

Take care of business and watch your dreams unfold before your eyes.

Make prayer part of your dreams!

LOVE

Encompasses all

LOVE

LOVE WILL TAKE YOUR BREATH AWAY.

LOVE IS THE ACTION BEHIND THE WORDS.

LOVE IS YOUR AFFECTION WITHOUT PAYMENT.

LOVE IS TRUE BROTHERHOOD TOWARD MAN.

LOVE IS THE HOPE YOU WILL ALWAYS CHERISH.

LOVE AND PASSION WORK HAND-IN-HAND.

YOUR HEART AND SOUL IS THE CHEMICAL MAKEUP OF LOVE.

LOVE YOUR PARENTS UNCONDITIONALLY.

LOVE LOOKS BEYOND THE NEGATIVE ISSUES.

HAVE A LOVE AFFAIR WITH YOURSELF, AND IT WILL RUB OFF ON OTHERS.

I LOVE YOU.

PRAYER IS LOVE!

YOUR HEART

Your heart is the generator of your existence.

Your heart is the home of your spirit.

Your heart shows you how to love.

Your heart makes you loyal to others.

Your heart introduces you to courage.

Generosity and compassion is supplied from your heart.

The heart is the center of attention.

Use it wisely and always pray!

PASSION

Passion is your appetite for love.

Passion is your force behind your desire to succeed.

You must possess passion to follow your dreams.

Passion should be controlled and reflect your strong will.

Passion is your devotion.

Passion should be directed toward your goals.

Passion grows with your motivation.

Passion is your intense feelings of enthusiasm.

Passion has no borders. It's boundless.

Make every prayer passionate!

APPRECIATION

Be grateful for what you have and work toward the things that you want.

Appreciation brings out your true qualities as a person.

Be thankful and fully aware of this value.

Appreciation is a highly regarded gratitude.

Your life and how you live should be admired.

Appreciation has no price.

Appreciation is to acknowlege your surroundings.

Appreciate yourself and family.

Appreciate prayer!

SHARING

Your debt to society is to share what you have learned.

Don't let life pass you by without giving back.

Sharing is when you give a part of yourself away.

Love and respect is built around sharing.

Don't expect anything back. Sharing should never be equal. Sharing is from the heart.

Your family should inherit your knowledge.

Sharing has no property.

When you share, you want others to come into possession of your offering.

Share your thoughts with a prayer!

THANK YOU

Thank you is a simple expression with tremendous meaning.

Yes, you should be obligated to say thank you.

Thank you is more than gratitude.

It doesn't always take words to say thank you.

Giving is one of the best ways to say thank you.

Do you realize how powerful saying thank you is?

Don't miss your chance by not saying thank you.

Thank you is being graceful by bowing through words.

Don't make saying thank you hard.

Thank you for hearing my prayer!

RELATIONSHIP

Your most powerful relationship is with yourself.

There will never be a substitute for your parents.

Family will exist when everyone exits.

Establish friendship and hang on to it.

Personal relationship is a connection with trust and honesty.

Relationship is your association with kinship.

Relationship is your association with others that stamp your signature.

Relationship is each other.

Have a relationship with prayer!

JOY

Don't let anything take away joy.

Relax and smell the roses.

Pleasure and delight is an emotion you must always keep.

Talk with a smile. Life is less stressful.

Control pain and enjoy amusement.

Why not enjoy yourself. . . Just think of the other choice.

Freedom is your biggest enjoyment. Don't lose it.

Fill your life with joy.

Make sure joy is in your home.

Enjoyment comes with prayer!

SMILE

A SMILE IS THE GATEKEEPER TO YOUR SOUL.

WHEN YOU SMILE YOU LET PEOPLE IN.

A SMILE IS MORE THAN A FACIAL EXPRESSION. IT'S A WINDOW TO YOUR HEART.

ATTITUDES ALWAYS CHANGE WITH A SMILE.

USUALLY SMILES ARE SPONTANEOUS, THAT'S WHAT MAKES IT GENUINE.

EVEN A SILLY SMILE COUNTS.

A SMILE IS YOUR APPROVAL.

A SMILE IS A RELEASE OF YOUR EMOTIONS THAT MAY AFFECT OTHERS.

TURN A FROWN INTO A SMILE.

BE HAPPY – SMILE WHEN YOU PRAY!

FORGIVENESS

If you go through life without asking for forgiveness, you haven't lived.

True forgiveness harbors no resentment.

Forgive and forget.

Should you justify forgiveness?

Forgiveness is a removal of your shortcomings.

Forgiveness is asking for a pardon.

Forgiveness is your chance to make good on your mistake.

Forgiveness gives you inner strength and courage.

When you ask for forgiveness, you ask for tolerance and patience.

Forgive me for I have sinned . . . pray!

SEX

The opposite sex exhibits sexual interest when aroused.

Sexual intercourse requires thinking before acting.

Protection is a necessity for both parties.

Counseling from your parents and elders is especially needed.

Sex is private and personal. Don't make it a scheme.

Just say no—means no. Don't take it any further.

Most sex happens on instinct not love.

Sexual emotions are different between male and female.

Control your desires.

There is a difference between making love and having sex.

Having sex is taking no responsibility because who knows
what might happen nine months later?

Sex is natural like your "X" and "Y" chromosomes.

Reproducing is part of your existence.

Pray together!

THANKSGIVING

Thanksgiving is a national holiday to give thanks to family, friends, and life.

You are acknowledging those that have contributed to your well being.

This is your expression of gratitude toward others.

You make a personal account and credit those responsible.

Thanksgiving is an appreciation that should be shared everyday -- not one day out of the year.

We are all thankful for so many things.

Be thankful for what you have.

Thank your mom and dad.

I'm grateful.

Show gratitude with prayer!

FRIENDS

A friend will cry for you.

A friend will cry with you.

A friend will wipe away your tears.

A friend helps when he or she is not needed.

A friend is your conscious -- just ask.

A friend treats your mistakes as if they were his/hers.

One friend is worth millions -- two friends are. . .

Can you truly measure the price of friendship?

A friend is a marriage full of love without the intimate passion.

Make a friend with prayer!

FAMILY

Family is your most valuable asset.

Family is highly important.

When everything fails around you, you still have family.

Family is your guidance into manhood.

Family is your Rock of Gibraltar.

Family is your gladiator who will fight along side you.

Family will help you exceed your limits.

Family will love you unconditionally.

Never stop loving your family.

A family who prays together stays together!

RESPECT

Respect is a short word,

With

Big results.

Love thy neighbor with prayer!

PARENTS

You can live with one parent or two. It doesn't matter.

They are yours.

Mother, father, or guardian, they are irreplaceable.

Parents protect you from the world until you can protect yourself.

Parents are your source of origin that gave you birth.

Allow your parents to share their life experiences with you.

I guarantee you will grow wiser.

Make sure your relationship with your parents is worthy.

The best thing you can do is quote your parents. . .

Did you learn something?

When you pray for your parents, you pray for yourself!

RESPECT YOUR PARENTS

Success starts at home from listening to your parents.

Listen and obey, even when you don't want to.

Your parents are your foundation to your future.

They will lead you down the right path if you let them.

Your parents have experience. You don't.

Respect your parents and the whole world is yours.

Join your parents in prayer!

HAPPINESS

Happiness is the ultimate pleasure.

If you chase happiness, you are really sad.

Happiness is good fortune without a deposit.

Happiness is a gift, so take advantage of it.

Never justify happiness; indulge in it.

Happiness is a welcoming committee with grace.

Happiness is a blessing because we have so many faults.

When you share happiness, you share your spirit.

Happiness is a product we should all market.

You can live and die happy.   It's your choice.

A prayer a day will keep a frown away!

LIFE'S GIFTS

Something I want to say

LIFE AND DEATH

Life is the greatest miracle.

Death is the loneliest emotion you can ever experience.

Life's journey is not the same for everyone. We all have different paths to travel.

Death is the final destination.

Life is everything you can imagine.

Death is the mystery we all face.

Life is the sunlight that beams in our face.

Death is the darkness that we can not see.

Life is a celebration.

Death reveals the accomplishments of your life.

Life is joy and pain.

Death is pain and joy.

Life and death begins at inception.

Prepare for death while living with prayer!

CHOICES

Choices are unwritten rights inherited by you as a human.

This is your freedom to become who you are.

There are wise and unwise choices. It's your decision.

Ultimately you decide.

Sound judgment is part of your soul.

Poor judgment can be a mistake or intentional.

When you make a choice you control it.

Not all choices benefit you.

Always use wisdom when making a choice.

You have the choice to pray!

EGO

My ego is bigger than your ego.

Control your ego and you control your behavior.

Your ego is your doctrine that guards your
self-interest.

A conceited ego still needs plenty of room to grow and
develop.

Did I mean mature?

Did you make your ego your universe?

Your ego is your conscious talking out loud.

Have you ever met a beautiful egotistical person?

It's great to think highly of yourself within reason.

When you're obsessed with yourself, you lose yourself.

Your ego can define you.

 Pray unselfishly!

PEACE OF MIND

Peace of mind is when you rest your thoughts.
You take away all chaos and maintain law and
order in your mind.
Peace of mind is a pause of action and time.
Peace of mind is your reason to hesitate.
Peace of mind is putting yourself on timeout.
It is important to suspend your mind in silence.
Your mind deserves an emotional rest.
You must learn how to guard your consciousness.
You must teach yourself how to reach this process.
Prayer will give you peace!

DRUGS

Drugs have failure written all over it.

Stay pure and clean and your body will thank you as you grow older.

Many athletes have been associated with drugs, which have created negative results.

Drugs can poison your future.

The dark side of drugs is addiction.

Medicines for treatment are the only drugs you should use.

Illegal drugs are a substance you don't buy from the pharmacist.

Drugs can make your family and friends disappear.

Be addicted to prayer!

GROOMED

A well dressed woman is sexy. A well dressed man is handsome.

Staying neat and trim is your responsibility.

Cleanliness is next to godliness.

We look differently at a tidy person.

Groomed is having things in good order.

Certain conditions have to be met to have precise arrangement.

Grooming is a sense of design.

Being groomed is just a simple upkeep.

Your appearance attracts others.

A well groomed person feels good about him/herself.

A groomed person leaves lasting impressions.

It doesn't take skill to be groomed. It takes substance.

Tailor your prayers!

HAPPY BIRTHDAY

A birthday is a celebration of life.

Be grateful that you have lived another year.

Your 18th birthday is the gateway to manhood.

The ages 18-25 are critical to your independence and maturity.

Some say life begins at 18, while others say, you just reached one of your many milestones.

When you become older, you grow wiser.

Now it's time to share, grow, and determine your destiny.

Turn a page in your life with determination and goals.

Don't lose sight of your parents and others who have helped you reach this age.

Be excited about entering the known and the unknown.

This is a great day to give thanks. Pray!

CHANGE

THE ONLY THING CERTAIN IS CHANGE.

CHANGE IS GOOD, ACCEPT IT.

DON'T FIGHT CHANGE.

MAKE CHANGE WORK FOR YOU.

YOU CAN CHANGE YOUR BELIEFS.

YOU CAN CHANGE YOUR APPEARANCE.

JUST DON'T CHANGE WHO YOU ARE.

YOU CAN PRAY ANYWHERE!

CHARACTER

Character is your reputation that describes your qualities.

Character is the shadow that follows you around your whole life.

Character is your behavior that others judge.

Character is your moral strength to keep you honest.

Character is your unique trait that separates you from others.

Character describes your being.

Build character with prayer!

PERSONALITY

Personality is your most intimate affair made public.

It's a collective judgment of your character and behavior.

It's your everyday performance in person.

Personality is beyond your physical being. It's the makeup of your soul.

You shape your personality by your experiences.

Good sound reasoning makes your personality attractive.

You are the producer and director. . . Cut!

The role you play should win an Oscar, if your personality is shaped to serve.

Make prayer personal, pray!

LEADERSHIP

Take charge without reservation.

Make challenging decisions with integrity.

Get the job done.

Make your presence known.

Speak direct and to the point.

Gain trust and respect.

Be the person to count on.

Be able to do what others can't.

Lead with prayer!

MATURITY

Develop the mind.

Grow up to accept responsibility.

Distinguish between right and wrong.

Dependable and reliable.

Obligated to commitments.

Accountable for self.

Love and respect others.

You can grow and pray at the same time!

SPEAK

A person who says nothing gets nothing.

Speak and you shall be heard.

Talk and perform and you will be considered.

When you speak people listen.

If you're quiet no one will ever hear you.

The squeaky wheel gets greased.

No one will ever talk for you better than you for yourself.

Speak when you pray!

TESTS

A test is more than a pencil and paper.

Endurance becomes your overall grade.

Life's greatest rewards are always tested.

Your beliefs and convictions are your covenant to exhibit.

Your intelligence is your criterion.

Tests are how you react to the highs and lows.

Your diagnosis is obtained and examined by others looking at you.

You are always rated.

Raise your standards.

Trust prayer!

KNOW WHAT'S RIGHT

If you know what's right, you should do what's right.

You must practice this everyday.

Learn the rules and regulations of life.

Never walk away. Stand up and fight.

Live and learn.

Your life is part of the world and it will never change.

Giving is a gift.

Pray everyday. It works!

TOUGH TIMES AREN'T HARD TIMES
HARD TIMES ARE TOUGH TIMES

When you struggle with life's dreams, you work through the tough times.

Hard times are not having the things you need--not the things you want.

If you are living through tough times, make a change and see results.

Who said life is easy?

Tough decisions will create manhood.

Your path through life requires hard work and dedication.

Don't dodge your responsibilities--face them head on.

Tough times are tough if you make them tough.

Prayer can change things!

PROCRASTINATION

Procrastination can cause death to your soul.

Procrastination will keep you in a state of limbo.

Nowhere to go; nowhere to hide.

Procrastination is as wicked as the devil.

It's a formal commitment to nothing.

Eliminate procrastination.

Prayer offers many choices!

LIFE

Life offers many opportunities and the choices can be endless.

You only have one time in this physical presence to get it right. There are no encores.

Prepare to ride the rollercoaster of life. Hang on.

It's important to make your life worth living. Somebody's watching.

Never shorten your life; you owe it to the world.

Life is truly a miracle.

My life is part of your life. Will we ever get it?

Miracles happen with prayer!

LIFE'S GIFT

Life is truly a gift.

A gift is perceived from the mind and given from the heart.

Gifts say thank you…I appreciate you.

Each and everyone of you are gifts.

You will always know when someone needs a gift.

Everyday on earth is a gift.

Prayer is a gift for everyone

I MISS YOU MAMA

You laughed the pain away while you gave me the gift to cry for your suffering. I watched you cry and you gave me the gift to laugh by saying it wasn't that bad.

I was your gift and you were my gift.

Life didn't let you see how your gifts made me.

I miss you Mama.

CONGRATULATIONS

Dear Steve,

I am so proud of you and so is everyone else up in heaven too.

Love you,
Aunt Tootsie

Jordon is currently a sophomore attending a local college in Orange County, California. He intends to restart his baseball career after missing his first two years due to a shoulder injury.